Powerhouse Singing Techniques

Develop Your Voice's Power, Range, and Beauty

James A. Cohen

Copyright © 2017 by James A. Cohen
All rights reserved. This book or any portion thereof may not be reproduced or used in any manner whatsoever without the express written permission of the publisher except for the use of brief quotations in a book review.

ISBN: 9781521160374

Introduction

Welcome to the program! This book about voice lessons is unique, because I am going to give you the secrets that will turn your voice into the most amazing instrument it can be. These techniques are used by the world's greatest singers, and they are what make the difference between a good (or even great) singer and a world-class singer.

So, who am I? My name is James A. Cohen. I have taken voice lessons from the best voice teachers in history, from Italy to Germany, from the United States to South Africa, and even some remote locations in Belgium, France, and Denmark. These teachers were not chosen by chance; I went on a journey visiting the teachers of the best singers and most powerful performers in the world. My mission, which took me many years, was to seek out the finest and best of all vocal techniques. This I have done. But I didn't do it for me. I did it, (albeit many, many years ago) so that I could become an amazing voice teacher. And indeed, my students are some of best opera singers, pop artists, and country singers in America. Now that I no longer offer private lessons, I decided it's time to reveal my simple to understand, a bit harder to apply, yet fantastic result yielding methods, to you.

I've been reading books and buying online voice lesson downloads, CDs, and so on, for years, and I can say with confidence that the tips, tricks, and techniques I provide you with here are unique – and indeed, the most powerful ones in the world.

These techniques will work with any singing method. Perhaps you have a singing teacher or use a home study course. That will all work just fine in combination with my techniques.

This program will provide you with 19 techniques you need to start using right away. You can use them in conjunction with your regular voice lessons or home-study course, or even on their own. What I provide is technique, not a systematic approach. There are no scales, for example. But again, the idea is that you can use them with any method you are already using.

That said, this is not a program for beginners.

You can still develop your voice with other programs. There are great singers out there who have trained using all kinds of methods, but most of them used many of the techniques in this book, knowingly or otherwise. While you can still grow your voice without these methods, doing so would make your voice development slower than a turtle walking backwards.

Before we start … I no longer offer voice lessons. And I can't recommend voice teachers, but I can and will recommend a few home study courses. They are all good, and cost-effective. As I mentioned earlier, I've purchased a lot of online programs, so I know what's out there. For this list, I've narrowed it down to the three that, in my opinion, offer the most, are the most systematic, and yield the best results.

Here are my recommendations, in no specific order:

1. **Gil Magno's 2-DVD set**. I studied with Gil many years ago. Gil passed away in 2016, and he will be missed. But he left an amazing system called the Magno Vocal Course. He was a gifted teacher, and

it comes across in his vocal course. Go to www.amazing-singing-lessons.com.
2. Another great program is Roger Love's **"Set your voice free,"** which is a book and CD. The CD has some excellent systematic exercises. It is the cheapest, but also the shortest of these three programs. You can find it on Amazon.com.
3. **The Ultimate Truth About Singing**, a seven-week course, is probably my favorite of the three (a close tie with Gil Magno's course). The teacher is an old student of mine, and he adds a lot of value with his amazing approach, which, by the way, works very well with all of my techniques. It also covers many key aspects of voice development, from high notes to timbre to extreme vocal power. I've seen students make huge improvements to their voice that were shocking – even to me! Go to www.gumroad.com/l/SOXYJ

Here's to your success!

James

Table of Contents

Introduction 3
Technique #1 Warm-Ups are Super Important 8
Technique #2 You Must Exercise Your Voice Like a Muscle ... 12
Technique #3 Body Support 16
Technique #4 Breathing 19
Technique #5 The Secret to Developing Range 22
Technique #6 The Secret to a Perfect Tone 29
Technique #7 Use a Piano 36
Technique #8 Sing a Challenging Song after Every Practice Session 38
Technique #9 Singing New Songs 41
Technique #10 The Third Pillar of Singing: Calling Out 42
Technique #11 The Inside-Out Voice 46
Technique #12 How to Record Yourself 48
Technique #13 Change up the Routine 50
Technique #14 Resting the Voice 51
Technique #15 The Open-Throat Question 52
Technique #16 Supplements 54
Technique #17 The $795 Voice Maintenance Tool 57
Technique #18 Tongue-twisters – A True Voice Treat 60
Technique #19 Smartphone Apps 62
Looking Ahead 64

I recommend that you read the entire book at least once before trying any of the techniques. For example, the "Three Pillars of Singing" are spread throughout the book. Reading the whole book will give you a much better understanding of the full method and it will be easier to apply.

Technique #1 Warm-Ups are Super Important

If you start practicing without a proper warmup, you can hurt your voice. Not only that, you will be wasting your time if you try to grow your voice without a proper warmup. Only after your voice is warmed up can it start to grow and expand. Otherwise, whatever exercises you're doing to expand your range or improve your tone will only warm up your voice, but nothing more than that.

That said, there is a benefit to warming up your voice daily. Even if all you do is warm up, it will help your voice maintain any previous gains and stay in shape. There could be a slight improvement in the voice after a few months of warmups, but of course we want to expand its range and improve its tone.

So, how should you warm up your voice? In one word, gradually. Start by humming on a five-tone scale. Move up the scale one half a note at a time, and keep it nice and slow. Keep your mouth closed, but your top and bottom teeth far apart. This will set your voice in the right placement, and develop your resonance. Pretend you're chewing gum while humming with your mouth closed. Doing so spreads the resonance around so you get some nice tones from your hard and soft palate, as well as from your nasal cavity and jaw.

Only raise the notes to a place you're comfortable singing in. For men, start at low C and hum on six or seven scales, reaching the middle C or C sharp as the highest note. For women, start on the F above low C and go up six or seven scales, ending on an F or F sharp above middle C.

Here's one of my favorite warmup exercises. Do the hum again, but this time play it faster, and do the same scale twice – once with your mouth closed, and once with it open. Open your mouth only slightly; don't force it open. Let gravity drop it. The idea of this exercise is to train your voice to treat actual singing like humming. Nice and easy, almost effortless.

If you're familiar with lip rolls, do some of those, also on the same range I mentioned before. Don't go too high. Remember, this is the warmup, and remember the key word: gradual.

Now let's warm up the really low registers. Start at the beginning of wherever you began your humming warmup, and start lowering the scale one half note at a time. Go as low as you can on a five-note scale. 1-2-3-4-5, 5-4-3-2-1. But this time, when you hit 1 on your way back down, open your mouth and try to make the note a little louder, gradually. This will really wake up your chest register and diaphragm. We'll talk about this specific point in a later chapter.

Now that you've warmed up your lower register, let's start with some falsetto. Do some more five-note scales on falsetto, using a clean, clear but soft tone. Make sure not to stress your voice. Try singing different vowels such as ee, oo, and oh.

At this point, you should have warmed up for about 10 minutes. This is a good time to switch to full voice warmups – but take your time. You need a good 20 minutes to warm up, although 30 to 40 minutes is ideal. I know this might sound like a long time, but here's the thing: the more your voice is warmed up, the better it will respond to later exercises in this book that develop range, volume, tone, and control. That said, if you can only spare three hours a week to practice, it will be better spent on three days of practice – half an hour each time for warmup, and another half-hour on exercising the voice – than practicing for half an hour each day for six days.

So, back to the warmup. Now that we're doing full voice exercises, start with a simple four-note scale, 1-3-5-8, and back down. Start with an easy word like "nah," as in "not." Start at the bottom note and sing nah on the 1-3-5-8 and back down, going up half a note at a time. Keep it soft but clear, and only go as high as is very comfortable. If you start getting up there, feel free to blend the voice and slip into a light falsetto, but only if you can easily slip in and out of it.

Repeat this exercise, but this time on a "yaw," as in "yacht." Depending on how much time you have, repeat this again on "wah."

Lastly, do some octave jumps. You can do these humming, on lip rolls, on a "nah", or on all three. Start from a very low tone and work your way up, without getting so high as to strain yourself.

Now that you've warmed up properly, drink a room-temperature cup of water. Then, any exercise you perform at this point will have ten times the impact it would have had without the warmup.

Summary: Warmups are an often-overlooked part of practice – but it's crucial that you spend enough time warming up if you want to develop your voice. Warming up by itself is also beneficial to the voice, as it maintains the voice's youth, and can also have long-term development effects. A proper warmup is 20 to 30 minutes long, which should then be followed by a good 30 minutes of range-increasing exercises (more on those in a later chapter), tone development and so on.

Technique #2 You Must Exercise Your Voice Like a Muscle

This technique is something that some voice teachers do, while others tell you it's a bad idea. I believe the latter are either ignorant of how the voice works, or they simply want their students to stay with them forever.

Working your voice like a muscle means that you exhaust your voice. You don't hurt your voice by doing anything severe, but after the proper warmup, you exercise your voice until it gets tired. This is the same way you would exercise any muscle in the body. If you're trying to develop your biceps, you lift weights until your biceps get tired, and then some. Let's say you're lifting 15-pound weights. The first five or so lifts don't tire you out, nor do they promote muscle growth. But after a couple more, maybe 10 or 15, you start to feel tired, and that's when the muscle is provoked enough to start growing during the subsequent resting period.

The same goes for your voice. Unless you are a brand-new singer or have never taken a single voice lesson, you know the difference between a tired voice and hurt or strained vocal cords. I'm talking about the first – a tired voice. When your voice starts to get tired, that's when you're actually developing your range and tone.

So, the question is, how do you get to the point where your voice tires out fairly quickly? Easy answer! First, make sure you warm up. Then, all you have to do is exercise the voice at its limits. If, for example, you can sing to an E above middle C with ease, but you start to struggle with D, E, F, and F sharp, then those notes are where the magic will start to happen. Do as many exercises as you can up in those high notes. Do five-tone scales all around that area.

Don't forget your technique. We'll speak in a later chapter about bodily support, breath support, and overall singing technique. So make sure you're using all that while you're singing at the top of your range. This will ensure that you don't damage your voice. You simply want work it hard, to promote growth.

Now that you've reached that point of healthy vocal fatigue, how long do you need to exercise for? It depends on where you're at in your vocal training journey. If you've just begun, I recommend working in that condition for only about five minutes. But within a few weeks of proper warmups and working in that vocal fatigue sweet-spot, you can easily increase it to 10, 15, 20, and 30 minutes. As long as you're supporting the voice (as we will discuss in the next chapter) and breathing correctly (another chapter), working with vocal fatigue will only develop your voice and pose no risk whatsoever to your vocal cords.

On this point – and this is also the subject of an upcoming chapter – you also need to rest your voice after each vocal workout or voice lesson. What this means is that you need to warm down the voice for a solid five minutes, drink a large glass of room-temperature water, and then not talk or sing for about an hour. I know this sounds like a lot of work – but remember, you don't need to work out your voice every day. Really, the best thing for your voice is to have fewer workout sessions using better methods (such as the long warmups, warm-downs, resting afterwards and so on), as opposed to working out every day using only mediocre methods.

Another point we need to make here is that since the voice is a group of muscles, you will benefit from protein shakes after an intense voice workout. This has helped a lot of students recover faster from workouts and to make changes in their voices happen much sooner.

Find a good-quality protein powder. Avoid the cheap ones, as they are full of chemicals, sugars, and other ingredients you don't want in your body. I'm well aware that the better ones are more expensive, but you won't need to drink a protein shake every day, just on days you practice your voice, which should be 3-4 days a week.

Here's one last point on the idea that you need to exercise your voice like a muscle. Anyone who goes to the gym will tell you that you have to work out the whole body, not just the biceps or legs. Here too, you need to start (if you haven't already) focusing on your entire body's health. You need to do cardio, sit-ups, back muscle exercises, as well as abs and chest exercises. I won't go into any detail on those exercises, but if you consult either a personal trainer or a simple Google search you will find more than enough exercises for each of the areas I mentioned. There are always the machines you can use in the gym, but there are also simple ways to get the same results at home, so don't feel obliged to sign up for a gym.

Summary: Treat your voice – or, more importantly, the way you develop your voice – as a muscle. Don't be afraid to work it until your voice is tired, and then stay in that vocal fatigue zone for a while. Exercise your full body, do cardio, sit-ups, weight training, and stretches. Take your time with your voice. Arnold Schwarzenegger didn't build his body in a day.

Technique #3 Body Support

This technique is the first of the three pillars of singing. While all the techniques in this book are important to the development of your voice, you need to apply only three of them when you sing – techniques #3, 4, and 10.

If you've been singing for more than a day, I'm sure you've heard about support. Some teachers swear by it, some never mention it, and most are simply confused about it. Here's what I learned from my teachers and what has worked for thousands of my students.

First, let's begin by explaining what support is. Imagine you're pushing a car from behind. The motor is not working, so all you have is your strength. You can probably last for an hour at the most. That is what your vocal cords are. Standing alone, they can do the job, but it's strenuous. Then someone comes along and starts pulling the car from the front; now you are not only moving the car faster, with more control and more ease, you can also last much longer than you could alone. That's what support is.

So how does one support his or her voice? As I mentioned in the introduction, there are really seven methods for support, but the best of them all is abdominal support. This is the same sensation you feel in the bathroom, when you're taking a poop. You push your stomach outwards and downwards. Of course, you need to start with a good breath, and we'll cover exactly how to do that in a later chapter. But once you've taken that breath, apply support and start singing.

One of the many reasons that abdominal support is superior to other methods is the fact that you can adjust it for volume and tone. When you want to hit a higher note, achieve greater volume, or maintain a note for longer than usual, simply *push* harder. You're already pushing with a fair amount of pressure, so the increase might be only slight, but it will still deliver the desired effect.

Another reason I favor this method is because nobody can tell that you're doing it. Some other methods include raising your chest, but this not only looks odd; if you lower your chest in the middle of a sentence, your chest will hit your lungs and push out way too much air – and that is noticeable!

I could go on for hours about the pros and cons of the various methods, but for the sake of practicability, let's keep it simple. Abdominal support is the easiest method (you already know how to do it), and yields the best results. Your voice will sound fuller, richer, and smoother. You will have more control over your voice, and you will preserve your voice for the rest of your life. I've met many old people who can barely walk, but their voices are as strong as a 25-year-old's, and they all use abdominal support.

Doing sit-ups will also help you develop better support, as will working the muscles of your chest, lower stomach and back.

Lastly, support will make your voice more reliable. Sometimes I hear singers say how some days they "just can't wake their voice up." Support is like the ignition of a car – it will wake your voice up, and keep it running. So don't push the car all on your own. Your voice will thank you.

Summary: Support is essential to the voice. The best support method is simply pushing the stomach outwards and somewhat downwards, as you do when you're going to the bathroom. This will keep your voice healthy, strong, and give your voice the round, consistent tone that every singer wants.

Technique #4 Breathing

This is the second pillar.

Breathing, of course, is very important for singing. And while singing is exhaling, the inhaling process can make a huge difference to the sound of your voice.

So what is the secret to breathing, you ask? Great question! The secret to breathing is that you must breathe into your lower stomach, the side of your stomach (also known as the love handles), and into your lower back. Breathing in this way will make your voice sound smooth, consistent, and rich!

Here's what you need to do. Sit at your desk or table, placing your arms in front of you, and put your head down towards your arm, as if you were going to take a desk nap. Don't put your head completely down, just about half way. Now, take a deep breath through your nose, and notice how the air fills your lower back and sides. Take a few more breaths, nice and slow, and really start to get the feeling of what it's like when the air fills up all the right spots.

Now practice this standing up. If you're having a problem getting the air into your lower back and sides, just sit back down and again go through the exercise. This might take a few practices, but eventually everyone can breathe correctly, and the changes you will experience once you've mastered this technique are, quite frankly, amazing.

Make sure that your chest rising almost imperceptibly. A little bit of rising is normal, but make sure it's not noticeable. This is because if you elevate your chest, it can then come crashing down and hit the lungs, releasing way too much air and creating a breathy, tired sound.

The main issue with any breathing method isn't so much understanding how it works or even doing it correctly; rather, it's how you use the breathing technique while singing. This can take time and practice to overcome, because you've probably been breathing incorrectly for many years.

Start by practicing only with the breath. After about a week or so, incorporate it into your warmup as best you can. And after another week or so, incorporate it into your singing as well.

The second stage of this method is to make it second nature, so that you don't need to think about while singing. Making this a habit will ensure that you have a high-quality tone and free up your mind to focus on other aspects of singing – namely, the words and feeling. The more room you have in your conscious brain to dedicate to aspects of singing that really do need in- the-moment thought, the better.

Lastly, once you've taken the correct breath, don't forget to support the voice as we spoke about in chapter 3.

Summary: The correct breathing method, used by all the world's greatest singers, involves breathing into the lower stomach area, love handles, and lower back. The chest and shoulders should not move almost at all, especially not the shoulders. Practice this method of breathing until it becomes second nature, and don't forget to support the breath using the method of support covered in chapter 3.

Technique #5 The Secret to Developing Range

This is probably the most often asked question. How do I develop high notes? (Though to be honest, I think the most important question is about how to develop a superb *sound*, and I will answer that question in the next chapter.)

So let's tackle the range question. As you will see, it's not that complicated.

To develop range, you must do two things. First, you must access the high notes with falsetto alone. As long as you can sing the notes in falsetto, you can develop them into full-blast, ear-shattering-opera or rock-sounding notes. No fake "head voice" or anything that tries to cut the fun out of the notes.

Most people I've encountered could indeed sing up to a high C (male high C and female high C) and higher in falsetto, even if they were very weak and unsupported. The key here is that your vocal cords can achieve the right coordination of those notes – and as long as you can sing a note in falsetto, your vocal cords are capable of forming the right coordination.

The second thing you need to do at that point is strengthen those notes until they become full-blown high notes. I'll explain how to do all of this shorty.

But first, remember that high notes are not a separate entity in the voice. It's all one voice. And you need good technique to expand your voice. We're covering what good technique is thoroughly in this book, so you need to use all the techniques in this book if you'd like to develop your high notes to their maximum and still maintain a beautiful, sexy sound.

Let's start with the actual techniques. As I mentioned, first we need to access those high falsetto notes. Sitting at your piano or keyboard, take a good breath (chapter 4), support the sound (chapter 3), and sing along in falsetto as you play a 5-tone scale. Start at the high end of your range, and keep it light and easy. No need to strain the voice at all. Any notes that cause you to strain are notes that are not developed quite yet (but you will conquer those, too).

Next, start the five-tone scales a few notes below your high range, so that you start the singing in full voice and transition into falsetto on the higher notes. This can be tough for many people, but it's really just a matter of practice. You can also practice this on a full octave scale, where the bottom two or three notes are full voice and the higher ones are in falsetto. Start the bottom notes lightly; you don't want to start with a full loud note and then transition into a soft falsetto note. That can be hard, and is also not helpful.

You'll need to do a few things to strengthen those falsetto notes. For one, you'll simply need to get comfortable singing falsetto. Some of you may have already been singing for years in falsetto. For some of you, this may be a new experience.

I know singers who have chosen a two-week period and spoken only in falsetto. It drove everyone crazy, but it got their voice super comfortable in that range. I don't think you need to do that, but do start to sing in the shower in falsetto and on every occasion you can.

After about a week or trying just the simple five-tone scales and octaves, we'll focus on individual notes, one at a time. Let's say the highest note you can sing comfortably right now is a G sharp. Start with a G in falsetto, on an "e" vowel. Hold it for about 10 seconds. Remember to take lower stomach, love handles, and lower back breaths, and to support the tone. Now just live in the world of the falsetto tone. Start soft, and try to hold it as steady as you can.

If you felt the tone was shaky or rough, start again. Remember, this is a slow process. Only once you feel the tone is good should you move on to the next one.

Move up and down the notes. Don't strain, but do push yourself a bit. You can do this a few times a week while practicing, but also as an exercise on its own, as long as you warm up beforehand.

Next, let's strengthen the falsetto notes even more. Hold onto a note, starting very softly on an "O" vowel as in "toe" – or an "e" vowel as in "eat", or an "ah" as in "awe" – but gradually raise the volume until you cannot raise it any more. Make sure you stay in falsetto and not go into full voice. Hold onto that loud volume for a second or two, then come back down. This exercise is known as "mezza di voce", and it is a 400-year-old Italian voice exercise. It will give you tremendous control over your voice and will develop your volume and tone nicely. But the reason I want you to do it is to develop the falsetto.

This might take you a few weeks, but the time you put in now to develop your falsetto will really pay off later when you will develop your falsetto into full voice.

Hopefully you can put in a good three weeks of practice. Your falsetto should be pretty strong now. Now we're going to do three things. One, you're going to continue to work on your falsetto. After a proper warmup, get into your falsetto for about five minutes. By this point, that should be easy.

Second, you need to do two main exercises in full voice. The first one goes like this: start in falsetto. It can be a fairly low note for your range, one that you can easily sing in full voice. Start singing the tone on an "oo" sound (as in "toon", or on an "oh" as in "owe"). Singing these exercises on an "oo" and on an "oh" is extremely important. This will ensure that the note develops correctly and sounds beautiful.

Start the tone (an "oo" or "oh" sound) in falsetto, and slowly raise the volume. As soon as you start raising the volume, you also need to start transitioning into full voice. For some this comes naturally; for others, it takes more time to develop. But if you've worked on your falsetto for a few weeks and have been warming up your voice all along, it should be in good enough shape to do this exercise smoothly.

Once you've reached a full voice and are comfortably singing loudly, start descending in volume until you're back to a falsetto.

Now start to go up the scale one half note at a time, alternating from an "oo" sound on one note to an "oh" sound on the next one. The exercise will gradually get harder as you get higher, so don't forget your breathing and support.

Go up the scale as high as is comfortable, and then back down. If you're feeling strong, do a second round.

Here's a quick summary of this exercise:

1. Take a good breath (technique #4)
2. Start on a tone you can easily sing in full voice.
3. Start the tone in falsetto.
4. Sing it on an "oo" or "oh" sound.
5. Slowly raise your volume until you start transitioning into full voice.
6. Do your best to keep that transition smooth, without cracks or breaks.
7. Continue raising your volume until you're fairly loud, but still at a comfortable volume.
8. Now bring the volume back down slowly, until you've transitioned back into falsetto.
9. Take another good breath, raise the tone by half a note, and repeat.

What this exercise does is take all the hard work you've done on your falsetto and turns those falsettos into full notes. Because the coordination of those notes is now second nature due to your strengthened falsetto, all you need to do is now strengthen your vocal cords a bit more and get used to singing those notes in full voice.

The second exercise is very similar. The only difference is that you start the note in full voice, rather than in falsetto. But the rest of the exercise is the same. Again, take a good breath. Start the note on an "oo" or "oh", at a very low volume. Then gradually raise the volume until you reach a fairly loud level, and then decrease back to the initial low volume.

Now, you may decide that the first exercise is all you can handle for the time being, and that's fine. Do a few weeks of that, then start with the second one. Either way, give yourself some time. Don't rush it. The voice needs time to grow and develop properly.

Now that you've done all this work – namely the falsetto exercises, the falsetto to full voice, and full-voice exercise – you should have a very strong voice and easy access to high notes. At this point, I would recommend using one of the three programs I recommended in the introduction so that you can apply your new voice to scales, and really connect all your registers. It's not that the exercises here haven't done enough for your voice already, but it would be a good idea to even out your voice with scales, which is something I cannot provide here.

Summary: Start developing your range by working on your falsetto. Follow the exercises in this chapter, and do so for a few weeks. Next, continue to do the falsetto exercises, but then add two more exercises: the falsetto to full voice and back, and the full-voice exercise. Do this for another few weeks. All along, make sure you breathe correctly, support the voice, and sing challenging songs after each workout (technique #8).

Technique #6 The Secret to a Perfect Tone

To me, this is the most exciting chapter. As I mentioned, while high notes are powerful, even magical, I believe the most important aspect of a singing voice is the tone or basic sound of the voice. High notes with a lousy sounding voice won't do you much good – but a gorgeous, elegant sound without high notes will still get you noticed.

I only mention all of this because as a singer, you should take control of your voice development. What you want to work on and how you want to prioritize your training is up to you, so I recommend focusing a lot more on the basic sound of your voice than on any other part of it. And lastly on this point: let's not forget that the proper voice techniques work together. Working on your breathing will help with tone, range, and power, as will the right support and so on.

Let's get to it. How does a singer develop amazing sound? The formula is easy to understand, but a lot harder to implement, and that's mainly because of the consistent effort and dedication it takes to get there. Let's start.

There are really only three elements. The first is simple: follow all the techniques in this book. The breathing, the support, working the voice like a muscle, as well as the techniques we will cover in the following chapters (such as resting the voice and singing a challenging song after every practice session).

The second element is creating an even voice using all three registers – namely, head, chest, and middle voice – and third, releasing stress from the body and voice.

Let me explain these two elements in more detail.

Creating an even voice means that you need to focus your exercises on all three registers. Most voice students, and indeed most vocal coaches, only focus on the head and middle voice. You will hear a lot of voice teachers say things such as "You have to work on the middle voice if you want to sing high notes," and the like. The problem is that all this talk about the middle voice has left a huge gap in the student's voices: the chest voice. Students and singers can go for years without ever practicing the chest voice, and this is a huge mistake. Not working on the chest voice not just leaves it undeveloped, but also denies the rest of the voice the richness it has to offer.

Think of the voice as a choir. You have bass, bass-baritone, baritone, tenor, countertenor, contralto, mezzo-soprano, and soprano. While each voice alone sounds amazing, together they sound heavenly. That's because they all blend together to create a much richer and fuller sound. And that's the goal for your own voice. When you develop your own bass, or chest register, along with your middle and head voices, your three voices blend together to create a much richer, fuller, and sexier voice.

I'm sure that you now see why focusing only on head and middle voice is a problem. So now let's talk exactly how to work on all three registers for the best results when it comes to blending voices.

First, if you've ever taken voice lessons, whether in person or through an online course or CD, you've probably worked on your head and chest a lot. Now it's time to work for a while on your chest voice, just long enough for it to kick in and start blending, and then you can start working on all three.

Start by simply singing five-tone scales, starting from your low range and then going lower. Most male students, for example, start practicing from the low C, but never go below that. Start there. Now, the low C is the highest note you're going to sing for a couple of days. Really engage those low notes. Feel the sort of rumbling in your belly. Let those vibrations free, as this starts the blending process. You can sing the five-tone scales on a hum, or with an open mouth.

We spoke about the *mezza di voce* exercise in the last chapter. For the low notes, the change won't be nearly as dramatic, as if you're not a bass it can be very difficult to raise the volume on those really low notes. But try starting soft, and raise the volume as much you can comfortably, and then go back down.

You will most likely also feel some vibrations in the chest area, which is great. But I want you to go lower in your range until your belly is engaged. You most likely won't sing in those notes in a song, but the whole point here is to blend the voice so that the richness of the low registers kicks in.

After a few practices of just the low notes, start blending all three registers together. You can do this in a couple of ways. You can sing 8-tone scales, which would be 1-3-5-8-3-5 and back down. You can sing them on "nah" as in "not," or on a "ya" as in "yacht." But keep these scales nice and easy. What you don't want to do is start at a low volume and then raise the volume on top. That won't help much for blending purposes. It's much better to start off with a soft sound at the beginning and maintain that tone throughout the exercise. Don't worry if you can't hit the high notes; the purpose of this exercise is to blend.

Another great scale to blend the voice is 8-5-3-8-1. Starting with a C, it would be C-G-D-back up to C, then back down to the lower C. You can sing these on any vowel you like, or on a lip trill. Again, maintain an even volume and focus on the blend.

Incorporate these sorts of exercises in every workout you do from now on. They are important. They will also make the high notes easier to sing, but that's just an extra benefit.

Another simple exercise you can do anywhere is simply to sing "ooh-ahh", with the "ooh" on a high note and the "ahh" on the same note, but an octave below. Keep it nice and slow and sing it with an easy, soft tone. Close your eyes, and visualize a can of blue paint being mixed with a can of yellow paint, or any other two colors. Just imagine that mixture happening easily, harmoniously, and beautifully. Feel free to pick a different metaphor to think about, but this one works well.

Now that we've covered the overlooked lower chest and belly registers, let's move to the head voice, i.e. the falsetto. The falsetto also contains a concentration of richness that should be blended with the voice. To do this, sing a note in falsetto on a "wah" sound (as in "wallet"). This is a very easy and open sound, and makes for great blending. Now slowly lower the tone until it becomes full voice. This is the practice of blending the head or falsetto voice with the full voice, and it can enrich the voice significantly. You can do this exercise two ways. After starting the note in falsetto, you can either lower the tone until the voice naturally turns into a soft, but still full voice. Or, you can stay on the same note, but slowly transition into full voice. Either way you will achieve the purpose of blending. Doing both versions of the exercise would be a great idea.

There is one more helpful tip for blending the voice, but I'll leave that for the next chapter. Meanwhile, let's get into the second, much harder aspect of creating a perfect sound.

The second element of a perfect sound is having a completely stress-free voice. This is easier said than done. Using the other techniques in this book will help with that, but you really need to find a way to release a lot of stress from your mind and body. I will give you some recommendations, but feel free to do some research on your own.

The best way I know to release stress is meditation. Transcendental Meditation, or TM® for short, is known to be one of the best methods in the world. There are alternatives such as mindfulness meditation, and others. Find one that works for you.

Some people relieve stress simply by listening to a great piece of calm music while wearing headphones. Others relieve stress by going for a walk or hike. The main thing is that it must be done daily. No matter what your method of choice, do your absolute best to make it a daily habit.

Just like eating or showering or using the bathroom, the body needs a daily dose of relaxation. Sleeping is not enough. You must add a relaxation session every day.

All the best singers in the world follow a relaxation practice of one kind or another. There is simply too much stress in our daily lives to allow it to build up. Some people think that all they need is an annual vacation to release their stress. Imagine a plant that needs one ounce of water every day. But instead of watering it every day, you wait for 128 days and then water it with one gallon of water. See the problem with that?

Your body and your voice are one and the same. You need a small dose of relaxation daily, not a huge dose at the end of the year. Not to say there's anything wrong with vacations, but don't let them fool you into thinking you don't need to relax during the year.

One effect of meditation is that it lowers cortisol levels in the body. There are also some supplements you can take (such as vitamin C) that lower cortisol, and I will cover more of them in a later chapter about supplements.

There are also ways to incorporate relaxation techniques into your vocal practices. For one, use the exercise I mentioned in the chapter about warmups, where you sing a five-tone scale twice on one breath, first on a hum and then with an open mouth. This trains the voice to treat singing as humming: with that same relaxed, easy production quality.

And to reiterate: use all the other techniques in this book, as they will help you have a stress-free voice. Supporting the voice with the stomach support, breathing correctly, and warming up well before singing all help support a healthy, stress-free voice. But again, you also need to be involved in *active* stress release, via a daily practice.

Summary: The secret to building perfect tone has three components. One, follow the techniques in this book. Second, blend your three registers – namely the head, middle and chest – and even what some call the belly register (those super-low notes that make your belly rumble). And third, conduct daily relaxation sessions – which, by the way, will help not just with your voice, but also provide you with better concentration, more energy, better moods, and much more. Follow these three steps, and you'll be well on your way to having the most incredible sound you could ever hope for!

Technique #7 Use a Piano

As we've spoken about earlier, what makes the voice sound magical is its overtones. That is, when all three, or even four registers blend together to create one voice. If you listen carefully, you can hear overtones of the other registers, as you can hear when a choir sings.

An important way to develop those overtones is by using a piano to train the voice. The piano is a string instrument. Even when you play the highest note, some of the lowest notes vibrate along with it. Play a note on the piano somewhere in the middle, listen carefully, and this becomes clear; you can hear the main tone along with the over- and undertones caused by the vibrations from the other strings.

And that is how our voice should work, too. Therefore, practicing with a piano helps the voice copy that great sound.

I'm sure that a lot of you practice with CDs or online voice lessons. While these can be beneficial, one of things they lack is that live, full sound of the piano. Even if they use a piano on the CD, it doesn't have the same effect. I'm not telling you to go out and buy a piano, as they can cost thousands of dollars, but if you have access to a good, well-tuned piano, use it. And if you're looking for a voice teacher, try to find one who uses a real piano, not a keyboard.

Lastly, listening to a high-quality piano soloist can be beneficial if you pay attention to the overtones and overall quality of their sound.

Summary: The piano is the ideal instrument to use for voice lessons or practice. When you realize that your voice is similar to the piano (in that it should be rich with overtones), it will help you blend the voice more naturally and beautifully.

Technique #8 Sing a Challenging Song after Every Practice Session

This is yet another crucial part of developing the voice, and one that's overlooked by many voice teachers.

Simply put, after every voice lesson or individual voice workout, you simply must sing a song so that the techniques and training you just practiced can become an integral part of your singing voice, and not just part of your exercising voice.

I know that might sound weird, but I've seen students who have had two voices: a singing voice and a voice-lesson voice. The latter was always much better than the first, because they simply never practiced their singing voice. Again, I know it sounds crazy, but it's absolutely true.

The reason this happens is clear: the students don't sing full-length songs after their lessons, so when they do sing a song, muscle memory kicks in and they sing it the same way they've always sung it.

And just as the problem is simple, so is the solution. You must sing a full-length song for at least five minutes (but ideally up to ten minutes) after every practice. But not just any song – it needs to be a challenging one. All you have to do to make it challenging is to start the song a few notes higher than you usually sing it, or sing along with a recorded song that's higher than you're used to.

The benefit from this is twofold: one, you incorporate the gains you've made from the exercises into your regular singing voice, and two, you achieve the healthy vocal fatigue we spoke about in the second chapter. This is simply invaluable, and it's one of the main reasons why so many students are unsuccessful with voice teachers. Those teachers are afraid to tire a student's voice out for fear that the student won't come back for more lessons, or because they don't want to develop their student's voice too fast (for the same reason).

I recommend having a playlist of songs that you already know are too high for you – at least for now, that is – so that you don't have to waste time after a practice session finding a song and deciding whether it's the one you want to sing right now.

As you're singing the songs, don't forget your main technique, which is the breath and the core support, although before we finish we will know of one more fundamental technique.

After about 5 to 10 minutes, or perhaps less at the beginning, you will achieve vocal fatigue. But remember, your voice will then heal and be stronger than before. It usually takes a few hours for the voice to heal if during that time the voice is rested (i.e., no singing or speaking) and if you drink room temperature water or lukewarm tea with honey and or lemon. Without this sort of break, the voice will heal and become stronger in about 24 hours, which is usually after a good night's rest.

Summary: An often-overlooked but incredibly important way to develop the voice is to challenge the voice, after every practice session, with a song sung at a higher key than normal. Doing so for 5 to 10 minutes will yield powerful results and should be a common practice.

Technique #9 Singing New Songs

This technique applies to both the songs you sing after a vocal workout, as well your singing in general. The idea is that you need to sing new songs all the time. The benefit of this is twofold. For one, you will widen your repertoire. But the larger benefit is that you will be free to develop your voice once you rid yourself of old muscle memory.

You see, when you sing songs that you've been singing for a long time, you revert to old technique because of muscle memory. Eventually, after your new technique is strong and has overcome all your old habits, you return to singing older songs. Just make sure you reestablish your technique so you don't return to your old technique.

Technique #10 The Third Pillar of Singing: Calling Out

This technique is the third pillar of singing. It is the way you actually sing. The first two pillars were breathing and support. This one involves how you can actually release your voice in an elegant, commanding fashion.

The technique is simple, but takes a bit of getting used to. First, let's start with an analogy. Fill in the blank: Singing is to speaking as running is to _____. Did you guess walking? You are correct. While there are some technical differences between walking and running, running is really just fast walking.

The same goes with speaking and singing. Here too, there are a few small differences between speaking and singing, but singing is really just prolonged speech.

Try this. Say the word "no". Say it as if you were saying no to a supersized meal at McDonalds. Now again say no, but hold on to it a bit longer. Now again, but this time hold onto it for about 3 seconds. You can start to hear yourself singing. Maybe it sounds a bit dull, but don't worry.

Finally, I want you to say no as if you're calling it out to someone across a wide street because they're about to fall in a ditch. Really work up the nerve and, while supporting, hold on to the "no" for a good five seconds. Let your voice ring! Again, imagine that you're calling out to someone across the street.

The reason for that is because when you do need to call to someone who is far away, your stomach will contract to help support your voice. When you can see exactly how far away the person is, the brain can calculate how much support you need and contract the stomach in a way that will produce the perfect sound.

But you don't need to really see the person across the street. Simply imagining it will do the trick. The brain can't tell the difference reality and imagery, which is why, for example, if you watch a video of someone on a rollercoaster, your stomach will have the same reaction it would have if you were on said rollercoaster.

The main technical differences between speaking and singing are the vibrato, the length of time you hold each syllable, and the range of tones you use. While speaking, we still hold onto notes for a bit, but in singing we do it longer. We also use a wide range of notes while speaking, but in singing it is usually an even wider range. Vibrato is really the only thing we should be doing while singing, but don't do at all when speaking.

Back to the technique. You absolutely must retrain your brain to think differently about singing. "Singing" sounds hard. But "prolonged speech" sounds a whole lot easier. And it's not just a play on words. Singing really is prolonged speech. In fact, it's when we think of singing as "singing" or as "belting" that it becomes difficult. That's because when we think of it as anything other than prolonged speech, we *try* to sing, we *try* to make our voice sound like something it is not. And that is where we go wrong.

Instead, focus on speaking, and just hold the notes for longer. When you want to sing high notes, focus on calling out to a friend across the street. This will raise your voice is a healthy and supported manner.

I recommend that you listen to any of your favorite singers on the radio. You'll start to notice almost immediately that they are indeed just speaking the words, not "singing" them. Even opera singers use this technique, although they must add much more vibrato. But other than that, it is really just speech.

Now, I realize that this can take some time to wrap your mind around, so take your time and do the following three things: think about the idea as a concept, experiment with your own voice while recording (more on how to record later), and listen to your favorite singers to see how they do it.

It may take a while for you to finally conclude that singing really is just prolonged speech. But once you do accept it, it will change your singing forever. And you will become the vocal powerhouse you are destined to be.

Lastly, you might notice that all of a sudden, your voice sounds different, maybe even dull. This is a good thing, and we will cover it in the next chapter.

Summary: Singing is prolonged speech. Lower notes are just like a conversation with a friend, although you would add vibrato. The high notes are just like calling out to a friend across the street. Imagery is important for this part, as thinking as though you really are calling to someone who is far away will cause your stomach to contract by just the right amount. This will take some getting used to, but the results will be amazing in the long run.

Technique #11 The Inside-Out Voice

As mentioned at the end of the previous chapter, once you start speaking your vocals, you might feel like you're sounding dull. This is good. Allow me to explain.

When we speak or sing, we hear our voice from inside our own head. But other people hear us differently. Of course, what matters is how other people hear us. You can't fill up the audience yourself. You need other people for that, my friend.

But here's the thing. Not only do we hear ourselves differently – we hear ourselves the opposite of how others hear us. When we hear a full, ringing, vibrant tone, others hear a hollow, dull, boring tone. When we hear a dull, wide, non-attractive tone, others hear a sexy, elegant, amazing tone. It's just one of those things we have to live with.

What you're looking for, therefore, is to master the technique without worrying about the sound you hear. This can be confusing, but just remember that as long as you use correct technique – namely the breathing, support, and calling out – you will sound great.

Recording yourself can help you figure all of this out, but you must follow the technique I outline in the next chapter for that to work.

Summary: Your voice sounds much different to you than it sounds to others. In fact, it sounds pretty much the opposite. Aim for a voice that to you sounds full but dull, and focus on your technique more than on how voice sounds to you.

Technique #12 How to Record Yourself

Recording yourself is a very helpful tool for voice development. It can help you experiment with different techniques, track your development, and much more.

The problem is that most people don't know how to record their voice properly. And I'm not talking about the equipment. A smartphone will work just fine. But in order to record yourself accurately, you must follow a few guidelines.

First, you must record yourself in a room with good acoustics. It doesn't have to be Vienna's Musikverein or Boston's Symphony Hall, but it does need to have some sort of an echo, and not a lot of furniture or carpeting. This is because when the voice picks up on the acoustics, it really starts to shine. I've personally heard some of the world's greatest singers sing in a small room without acoustics, and it was not impressive.

Another way for the voice to shine, in addition to proper acoustics, is to have music in the background. I've heard countless voices with and without music, and the difference is incredible. (On a side note, keep this idea in mind when you're recording yourself and comparing it to your favorite singers on the radio; they have the benefit of a very expensive recording studio with some of the best voice technicians in the world. You have an iPhone.) So if you're comparing your voice with theirs, it's not a fair game. The only comparisons you should make is how your voice sounds today versus how it sounded a month ago and how it will sound a month from now.

By the way, even "live" singers at concerts have the benefit of a full studio and technicians. They're right there with them. And that is assuming the singer isn't lip-syncing (in other words just moving their mouth while the song is played from a CD). Even some of the greats like Michael Jackson would lip-sync, and many others. So give yourself a little latitude when it comes to critiquing your own voice.

Back to how to record yourself. We said the first rule is to record yourself in a room with good acoustics. The second rule is to stand at least 10 feet away from your recording device. And lastly, you need to face away from the recording device. I don't want to get into the science of these rules, but once you try it you will see that it makes your voice sound a whole lot better. And it's not that it changes your voice; it simply lets the recording device pick up on your true sound – the sound your audience will hear once you do make it to Vienna's Musikverein and Boston's Symphony Hall.

Summary: Recoding yourself is extremely helpful for voice development, but you must follow these three simple rules: record yourself in a room with good acoustics, stand at least 10 feet away from the recording device, and stand with your back to the recording device.

Technique #13 Change up the Routine

When it comes to routines, it's important to change them up once in a while. This is because the voice starts to get used to very specific exercises and stops to respond to them as well. This can take a while, though, so only worry about it once you've been doing the same routine for at least two months.

What I mean by "routine" is the actual exercises you are doing. Depending on your voice teacher or home-study course, you may be doing lip drills, one-syllable words like "goog" and "gug", or longer words on a full octave like "piano" or "mamamia". (By the way, the CD I recommended in the Introduction by Roger Love uses those googs and gugs, as well as some others, and the third recommendation, The Ultimate Truth about Singing, uses those pianos and mamamias as well as some others.)

So if you've been using one of these programs for, say, more than three months, it may be time to start using a different one – again, all in the name of switching things up. Then, after using a different set of exercises, feel free to return to the first one. If you give your voice a few months to try something else, when you go back to the earlier one it will again have a great effect on your voice.

Technique #14 Resting the Voice

This one is less a technique than it is an important aspect of voice training. You need to rest your voice after each practice session or voice lesson for a full hour. No talking. You also need to rest your voice periodically, meaning that if you practice every day of the week, you should give yourself a day off, preferably Saturday (there's research that suggests that Saturday is the best day for the body to recover).

Further, if you do have a heavy routine, meaning five or more hours a week, I would suggest taking off a full weekend once a month, and a full week every three months. During these rest periods it is okay to talk. But refrain from any singing or voice exercises, and try to keep speaking to a minimum.

Another aspect of resting the voice is drinking warm water with lemon – but I'll cover that in a later chapter.

Summary: Rest your voice after every voice lesson or vocal workout for at least an hour of no talking or singing. If you can't get through the hour without speaking, make sure you get a full night's sleep before you work out your voice again.

Technique #15 The Open-Throat Question

This is probably one of the most commonly asked questions. Do I need to sing with an open throat? The answer is yes and no. Let me explain.

Sure, there are times when the voice needs an open throat to make the right sound. But this needs to happen naturally. And it will, if you use the right technique.

As long as you are practicing the three pillars of signing – the love handles and lower-back breathing, the abdominal support, and the calling out method – your voice will work perfectly and respond to the needs of whatever tone you're trying to create.

I find that for many students, intentionally opening the throat only causes unneeded stress and doesn't make the voice sound better. Some students feel that it helps them, and I'll leave it to you to decide how it works for you. But don't forget that you don't hear your own voice the way others hear it, so make sure you record yourself (see chapter 12) before you decide.

Also, don't forget that the method here, and the one practiced by the greatest singers in the world, is to sing the way we speak. We don't speak with an open throat, so I see no need to sing with one. Similarly, as we mentioned in chapter 10, when you have a visual of a faraway person who you are calling out to, your stomach contracts by just the right amount. The same goes for the throat. If, for the tone and volume you are producing, and if it knows that it's right for your voice, your brain will instruct your throat to open by just the proper amount, the same way that it instructs the stomach. But if you're trying to open the throat, which is unnatural, it's almost as if you're trying to make your heart beat, and you don't need to.

Now, all that said, if you're with voice teacher who has been teaching you to open your throat, and it has been working well, then I see no problem doing that. As I was taught once by a doctor of chemistry, you don't argue with results.

Summary: The open-throat question is a common one. For most people, there's no need to intentionally open the throat. Opening the mouth will accomplish that, to the extent that the throat needs to be open. Experiment and see what works for you (i.e., what method sounds the best for your voice). I generally recommend that you not intentionally open your throat – but if it works for you, go for it.

Technique #16 Supplements

Nutritional supplementation can be very helpful for the voice, especially when you are not just maintaining the voice, but also growing it. I'll list the supplements that I've found helpful for either myself or my students.

As with all the supplements I list here, try to look for a good company. Their products will usually be more expensive than the other brands –but when it comes to supplements, you usually get what you pay for. Also, if you have the patience, try supplement at a time. This way you can see exactly how your voice responds to it.

Vitamin C. Vitamin C helps to keep your voice healthy because it keeps colds away, clears up mucus (make sure to get the non-acidic kind), and also helps lower your levels of cortisol, the stress hormone (which, as we noted earlier, is very helpful for the voice).

Zinc. Zinc lozenges are very beneficial for the voice. I take one after every voice workout, and it has always help me maintain a strong voice.

Coral calcium from Okinawa. Calcium – specifically, coral calcium, and specifically from Okinawa – is a very important supplement. It alkalizes the body and keeps colds away like no other supplement out there. You can probably take half the recommended dosage if cost is an issue. Alkalizing the body itself will help with your voice development as well.

Chlorophyll. Chlorophyll, in liquid form, is a very powerful voice aid. This is because chlorophyll disperses oxygen throughout the body and the vocal cords. This is definitely the best supplement when it comes to healing the vocal cords from fatigue, hoarseness and the like. It is also very helpful when developing the voice. Make sure to follow the instructions on the bottle, which usually direct you to mix a teaspoon or tablespoon of the liquid in a cup of water. If you can only afford or only want to take one supplement, I recommend this one.

Vitamin B12. B12 is extremely helpful because it helps to calm the body and voice. It is usually recommended that B vitamins be taken together, so look for a B complex.

Vitamin A. Vitamin A helps regenerate old cells into new ones. This can be very helpful for building your voice.

A good multi-vitamin can cover you for vitamins A, B, and C.

Now let's talk about a few things that are good for your voice, but are not considered supplements.

Lemon. Lemon mixed with warm water can make a huge impact on your voice. It clears out the throat and soothes the vocal cords. It also has plenty of health benefits. Feel free to mix in a spoonful of honey, as honey, too, is very helpful for the voice. You can drink a cup of lemon or honey water every day, or on days when you work out your voice, or whenever your voice feels tired or sluggish.

Protein. Protein is helpful when you are building your voice. We mentioned this in a previous chapter as well.

Exercise. Whether you use a treadmill or bicycle, you need to get your heart rate up and improve your cardiovascular health. This can have a major impact on your voice. Most people start hitting high notes with much more ease and have an easier time with vocal control and stamina after working out. Dancing is also a very helpful thing to do, as are cardio classes in the gym, because they change the tempo often, which benefits your breathing even more. If you're not signed up with a gym or lack access to a treadmill, just take a brisk walk. Once you start to realize the benefits you're reaping from the cardio, you'll be tempted to join a gym and take your health more seriously.

Water. Water is so important that it gets its own chapter. Stay hydrated until then!

Now let's talk about a few things that are bad for your voice.

Smoking. Need I say more? Smoking is absolutely horrific for your voice and for your health. Do whatever you can to quit, and please don't give me the BS excuse that you know someone who smokes and their voice is still okay. I'm not going to argue this point, so if you doubt the dire consequences that smoking will have on your voice, just Google it. Oh, and then stop smoking.

Drugs and alcohol. Drugs and alcohol are both awful for your body and your voice. I'm not talking about a cup of wine with dinner, but anything else can wreak havoc on your body and voice. Please, if you're engaged in either of these self-destructive behaviors, seek the help that is out there.

Caffeine. Caffeine is not great for your voice, but mainly because it dehydrates you, and that's bad for your vocal cords. But if you have it under control (i.e., if you're not drinking more than two cups a day) it's not the worst thing. Especially if you can increase the amount of water you drink. About an extra two cups of water for every cup of coffee is about right.

Ice cream, spicy foods, salt, eggs, carbonated drinks, nuts. These foods can all cause dryness in the voice, or excess mucus, which are both not good for your voice. The thing is that we all react differently to foods. For me, spicy foods don't cause any adverse effects on my voice, and if anything they help open my sinuses, which helps my singing. So when it comes to these types of foods or any other foods that may cause some people dryness or the like, simply experiment with your own voice and see what happens. And then, even for foods that do cause you dryness, what's really important is to not consume them before you sing or three days before a performance. If you're on the road singing every other night, it would be wise to cut out these foods completely, or at least until you get home and have a couple weeks to rest without singing.

Technique #17 The $795 Voice Maintenance Tool

About ten years ago, I had an interesting student come to my office. We'll call him Aaron. Aaron was a cantor in Frankfurt, Germany. He had replaced another cantor by the name of Yitzchak Meir Helfgot, who consistently hits high notes that rank him among singers with the highest male ranges in the world. He easily hits the high C as if it's middle C, and I have personally heard him hit an F above high C during a cantorial concert in New York. Needless to say, his voice is huge.

When Helfgot was cantor in Frankfurt, he took voice lessons from a professor in a small town outside of Frankfurt. Lessons were (at the time) $795 for two lessons. After Aaron took the position, the community paid for his voice lessons, and he went to the same professor Helfgot had gone to. This piqued my interest. "What did he teach you?" I asked Aaron, hoping to find out a few "secrets" to voice development that I hadn't learned yet.

"Well, we did a lot of warmups," he said. "And?" I asked. "We also worked on abdominal support," he continued. "I know all about support!" I said, eager to hear the real stuff. "He made sure we engage the chest voice in an effort to blend it with the rest of the voice." *You've got to be kidding – I know all of this stuff*! Finally, I said, "Aaron, certainly, for almost $400 a lesson, there's something he taught you that I don't already know."

"There is, actually," Aaron said. "The professor said to drink one cup of water, every hour."

That was surprising. Sure, I've heard about the power of water. There's a great book called "You're Not Sick, You're Thirsty", (which I recommend, by the way).

But a cup of water every half hour? That was news to me. I probed Aaron some more, but it turned out that the water tip was the only thing he learned from the professor. But he did have some further explanations about why it was so important to drink water so often. The thing is that the voice dries up quickly. And because the cords need water to function well, it's not enough to drink water a few times a day. It needs to be often. It's also not enough to drink 8 cups a day, as recommended by many nutritionists. It may be enough for the body, but the voice needs more than that.

Intrigued, I started to experiment. I drank a cup of water every half hour for about three days. I needed to pee constantly, but my voice became really powerful. I was hitting my high notes with so much ease it was ridiculous.

Because of the peeing issue, I continued to drink a cup of water only every hour. My voice felt just as good.

So that is my recommendation: drink a cup of water, or even just half a cup, every hour. If you're not training and don't have a performance coming up, feel free to cut back.

A lot of my students do this, with some variations. Some drink two cups every two hours, for example, or even one cup every two hours. See what works for you. Regardless of what you decide to do, just know that adding any amount of water to your daily diet will have a positive impact on your voice.

Technique #18 Tongue-twisters – A True Voice Treat

Tongue-twisters are often taught as a way to warm up your voice and loosen your mouth, tongue, jaw, lips, and cheeks. But they are *so* much more than that.

Tongue-twisters have a truly magical power to clean up the sound of your voice. This will improve your overall timbre and tone, which is the most basic sound of your voice, and obviously is critical for any singer or speaker.

Here are some tongue-twisters you can use, but you can also find a plethora of them online. Of course, as with most tongue-twisters, mine are neither grammatically correct nor do they make much sense – but they will twist your tongue!

Go through the list twice a day for a week. At that point, you'll probably know them well enough that they won't be as difficult, so start using another list of tongue twisters. All you need is four lists. Simply rotate between the lists every week. Here are some of mine:

1. She said she'll chill and she said she'll shine on this chilly shiny night.
2. Go gather great grapes with a green grin.
3. Fishing for fish or shelling for shells?
4. Kissing a krill on a kind carpet can cause chaos.
5. Two toads talked of tall termites and took two tigers to tango.
6. Nice Nancy and not so nice Nadia sung a song with Jessica on a super nice night.
7. Grasping sunshine. (Read 5 times.)

Technique #19 Smartphone Apps

If you have a phone with apps, look into downloading a few that measure tone and volume. I have an app called "Tuna Pitch" that tells me which tone I'm singing. On the side of the screen, there is a "confidence" scale (from 0-100%) letting me know exactly how on pitch I am. At the bottom of the screen, another meter lets me know the volume, in decibels, that my voice is producing. Students can use these sorts of apps to really gain control of their voice.

For this exercise, just try to stay on pitch for as long as you can, and try to keep the decibel meter at the same level. The more you do this, the more accurate your singing will become, thus improving your overall sound.

Start by focusing just on tone. Then focus just on volume. After you've done a lot of those, maybe 100 or more, see if you can focus on both tone and volume.

Other apps can help you on your journey of becoming a better singer. Some are sort of memory games with notes – for example, the game plays two notes, which you have to repeat. Then it plays three, then four, then five, and so on. Some games do the same thing but add a color to each pitch, so you can focus on the color while at the same time develop better tone memory.

In general, I'm a fan of using technology to improve singing skills. Of course, it doesn't take the place of a good old-fashioned piano and a solid voice teacher, so put the tech into perspective. But overall, anything you feel can help you become a better singer is worth a try.

Looking Ahead

Now that you've read the whole book, perhaps consider going through it again, just in case you missed any crucial details. Then start applying all the techniques and methods I've described – and you'll be well on your way to becoming the best singer you can be.

Made in the USA
Lexington, KY
23 August 2018